THE GROSS COOKBOOK

GOOEY BRAINS!

Susanna Tee

Illustrated by Santy Gutiérrez

sourcebooks jabberwocky

Published by Sourcebooks Jabberwocky, an imprint of Sourcebooks, Inc.

P.O. Box 4410, Naperville, Illinois 60567-4410

(630) 961-3900

Fax: (630) 961-2168

www.sourcebooks.com

Originally published in 2017 in the United Kingdom by QED Publishing, an imprint of The Quarto Group.

Library of Congress Cataloging-in-Publication data is on file with the publisher.

Source of Production: 1010 Printing Group Ltd.

Date of Production: May 2017

Run Number: 500L333

Printed and bound in China.

10 9 8 7 6 5 4 3 2 1

Acknowledgments

The publisher would like to thank the following agencies for thier kind permission to use their images.
AdobeStock: 49 (ballylocci); **Alamy**: 20 (Rob Walls), 28 (Ashley Cooper pics), 13 b (REUTERS), 13 t (epa european pressphoto agency b.v.), 16 t (imageBROKER), 31 b (Mark F. Henning), 31 t (Bjarki Reyr), 35 b (REUTERS), 35 t (Alex Hunter), 41 t (Michelle Gilders), 59 t (Top Photo Corporation), 9 b (Bill Bachman), 9 t (Suzy Bennett); **Getty Images**: 24 (ROMAOSLO), 38 t (JUNG YEON-JE), 56 b (W. Robert Moore); **iStock**: 38 b (WEKWEK), 45 t and b (ElenaMirage), 56 t (flyingrussian); **Shutterstock**: 16 b (Aedka Studio), 41 b (Katy Foster), 52 b (Peter Stuckings), 52 t (meunierd), 59 b (Ali Iyoob Photography).

MIX
Paper from responsible sources
FSC® C016973

Contents

⋆ = disgusting recipe

Prepare to Be Disgusted!

Do you like safe, familiar meal times, where nobody shrieks or wants to puke, and the food doesn't look like something out of a nightmare? Then you've opened the wrong book. Better put it back on the shelf now.

Still reading? Want to put some fun and excitement into cooking and fool your friends into thinking you've developed some truly disgusting eating habits? Great, then this is the book for you!

Get your gag reflexes ready and practice keeping a straight face—you're going to need both as you dig into this book of repulsive recipes. You can cook up these concoctions to gross out your grown-ups or freak out your friends, but the very best part is that the recipes are actually torturously tasty!

Gross Out Planet

There are two very different parts to this book. DO NOT get them confused, or you might end up with an even more disgusting dish than you'd bargained for. Hiding out among the recipes are Gross Out Planet features, where we spill the beans on some of the most bizarre and disgusting foods that are eaten around the world. We hope you have a strong stomach!

THE REVOLTING RULES

RulE 1

"DON'T BE MEAN: COME CLEAN!"

What does this mean? It means it's not polite to leave your poor old grandma thinking you've put an eyeball in her drink. Jokes are funny, but don't upset people and always own up that it's just a trick.

RulE 2

"IT'S MEANT TO LOOK DISGUSTING, NOT BE DISGUSTING!"

Put simply: always wash your hands with warm, soapy water before preparing recipes, and don't scratch your butt (even when you think nobody's looking).

RulE 3

"IT'S NOT A JOKE IF THEY CHOKE!"

This might sound obvious, but don't force your little brother, the school bully, or anybody else to eat one of your creepy creations. It's revolting manners. Plus, it's often much more fun to eat the tasty trick food yourself while watching your friends' disgusted expressions.

RulE 4

"DON'T START THE FUN TILL YOU TELL MOM!"

Last, but not least—you might be eager to get started making your gruesome grub, but you MUST ask permission from the adult who's in charge of you, and make sure you read the rules of the kitchen on page 62.

Squiggly Jelly Worms

With clumps of "soil" still sticking to their glistening, translucent bodies, these squiggling "earthworms" are sure to give your friends, or your poor grandma, the shivers. There are so many different pranks you can play with these realistic-looking, but secretly super tasty, worms. Your hardest challenge by far will be keeping a straight face as your pals shudder with horror!

WHAT YOU'LL NEED

- 4 packets of raspberry or strawberry gelatin (such as Jell-O®)
- 17 fl oz (500 ml) boiling water
- 7 fl oz (200 ml) cold water
- 8 fl oz (250 ml) heavy cream
- ¼ teaspoon green food coloring
- ¼ teaspoon red food coloring
- 100 bendy plastic straws
- 1 empty juice or milk carton

SLURP!

Making the worms

First of all, you need to make your worms. Make sure you choose bendy straws, because it's the bendy part that makes them look really lifelike.

1 Empty your favorite flavor of gelatin packets into a large, heatproof measuring cup or bowl with a spout.

2 Add the boiling water and stir until the gelatin has completely dissolved. Stir in the cold water until it reaches the 25 fl oz (750 ml) mark. Leave to cool until it is lukewarm.

3 While you're waiting for your gelatin to cool down, pack your straws into the juice carton, with the bendy ends at the bottom. If the straws don't fill the carton, bundle them together with some plastic wrap.

4 Once your gelatin is lukewarm, add the heavy cream and food coloring and stir.

5 Pour the gelatin into the juice carton, filling the straws. Put the carton in the fridge for 2–3 hours or overnight until the gelatin is set.

WARNING

Ask an adult to help you when pouring boiling water.

Making the soil

While your earthworms are setting, you can make the soil to serve them in. This part is really simple.

WHAT YOU'LL NEED

- 1 package of chocolate cookies, such as Oreo® cookies
- 1 large plastic zippered food bag

1 If your chocolate cookies have a cream filling, scrape it out.

2 Put the cookies in the plastic food bag, seal the bag or hold the open end closed, and break them into small pieces by thumping or rolling them with a rolling pin or crumbling them with your hands.

3 When you think your cookie crumbs are the right size to look like soil, put the bag of crumbs to one side, ready for the wriggly worms.

MMM... GRITTY

REMEMBER: You're not a bird. NEVER eat real worms!

COOK'S TIP

When choosing a juice or milk carton to hold your straws, it's best to use one that is tall and thin that you can cut to get the straws out once the gelatin has set.

SERVING SUGGESTION

Now for the really fun part! Invite your unsuspecting victim over for dinner and when it's time for dessert, present them with a platter of worms, all tangled up in a pile of soil. Yeeeeuck!

Or try hiding one in your sandwich or salad at lunchtime. Make sure enough worm is peeping out so that your friend will spot it. When they try to warn you, take a big bite and watch them cringe!

Putting it together

When your worms have set completely, it's time to squeeze them out of their straws.

1 Cut or tear the carton to get the straws out.

2 Hold a small bundle of straws under warm running water for a couple of seconds to loosen the worms from the straws.

3 Squeeze the worms out, one at a time, onto a plate or sheet of parchment paper, starting at the top end of the straw.

4 Repeat until all your worms are out of the straws.

5 Sprinkle your cookie crumbs onto the worms. Mix the worms up so that all of them get a good coating of soil.

TASTY TIP

These deliciously disgusting worms will keep in the fridge for up to 2–3 days in an air-tight container.

Chewy Caterpillars

Australia

If you ever visit a fancy restaurant in Australia, then you might come across dishes featuring witchetty grubs. Witchetty soup, for example, sounds intriguing, but it's actually live, wriggly, bulbous caterpillars floating in broth! Yuck!

For thousands of years, witchetty grubs have been a staple source of protein for the Aboriginal people who live in the remote, harsh environment of the Outback. Only they don't bother with the soup… The caterpillars are pulled out from the dry ground and eaten live and whole, squirming as they are chewed and swallowed!

A wriggly snack

It is claimed that witchetty grubs taste like almonds. Would that be enough to tempt you to chew on some caterpillars?

Chewy!

Cat Poop in a Litter Box

There are plenty of opportunities for mischief and pranks with these yummy chocolate kitty poops. Your friends and family are bound to feel sick when you dare them to take a bite, but for that extra pranking fun, be sure to eat a whole one first and watch them go green! Mmm, tasty!

WHAT YOU'LL NEED

- 6 ½ oz (185 g) all-purpose flour
- 1 ½ oz (40 g) cocoa powder
- 1 teaspoon baking powder
- 7 tablespoons (100 g) butter
- 6 oz (175 g) superfine sugar
- 1 extra large egg
- 1 teaspoon vanilla extract

makes about 35

Making the cookies

1 Ask an adult to preheat the oven to 375°F (190°C). Grease two large baking trays.

2 Sift the flour, cocoa powder, and baking powder into a large bowl. Cut the butter into small pieces and, using your fingertips, rub the mixture together until it looks like breadcrumbs.

3 Add the sugar to the mixture.

4 Break the egg into a small bowl and beat together with a whisk.

5 Add the beaten egg and vanilla extract to the mixture and mix together with a wooden spoon to make a soft dough.

6 Take small pieces of dough and roll into log shapes to make "poops" and mold into straight poops, curly poops, or blobby poops.

7 Put each poop onto the greased baking tray, leaving a space between them so that they have room to spread when they bake.

8 Ask an adult to help you put the cookies in the oven and bake for about 10 minutes until firm. Leave for 2 minutes to cool slightly and then put the cookies on a wire rack to cool.

Making the litter

While your poops are getting cold, you can make the "litter" to put them in. Serving your friend a cat poop snack is pretty gross, but go all out by presenting it on a dish of realistic-looking cat litter! This cat litter is really a delicious mix of soft cake and crunchy cookies to give it that authentic kitty toilet look.

WHAT YOU'LL NEED

- 1 unfilled vanilla sponge cake
- 2 packets golden Oreo® cookies
- 1 large plastic zippered food bag

1 Break the cake into a large bowl and, using your fingertips, rub together until it looks like litter.

2 Put some cookies in the plastic bag. Seal or hold the open end of the bag and hit with a rolling pin to make crumbs.

3 Repeat step two with the rest of the cookies until all the cookies are in crumbs.

4 Add the cookie crumbs to the cake crumbs and mix together. Now you're ready to add the poop!

TASTY TIP

These yummy cat poop cookies can be enjoyed immediately or stored in an airtight container for up to 14 days. This means you can make them in advance and have plenty of time to think up some gruesome and hilarious ways to prank your friends.

WHAT YOU'LL NEED

- 1 new, small cat litter tray or rectangular serving dish
- 1 new cat litter scoop or spatula
- a little light corn syrup

SERVING SUGGESTION

When a friend comes over, put the litter box on a sheet of newspaper and put it on the floor. Ask if they're hungry and pick up the tray and offer them a yummy poop! If they refuse, take a big bite from the cookie and tell them it tastes delicious.

Putting it together

It's time to serve up your toilet treat and this last step really increases the gross factor! The corn syrup makes the cookies shiny, giving them a very "fresh," squishy look. The cat litter tray will guarantee some memorable reactions!

1 Wash the new scoop and litter tray in hot, soapy water and dry them.

2 Using a pastry brush, coat the poops with a little corn syrup so that they look shiny in places.

3 Put the litter in the tray so that it covers the base. Put the poops in the litter, burying them slightly. Sprinkle a little of the litter over the top.

4 Add the litter scoop to serve the poops!

WARNING

Don't ever put your hands in a real cat litter tray. They are very unclean and could make you sick.

Civet Cat Poop Coffee

Indonesia

The world's most expensive coffee is also the most disgusting. Just like the coffee your parents drink, it is made from beans found in coffee "cherries." But there's a twist! Before the cherries are collected, they are eaten by the Asian palm civet cat, locally known as a *luwak*. Civets look like a cross between a monkey and a raccoon and live in Indonesia, where kopi luwak (Cat Coffee) is made.

The civet roams coffee farms at night and eats the best, ripest cherries. However, it cannot digest the bean in the cherry so, after a day and a half in its gut, the beans are pooped out. They are exactly as they were before, but now coated in yucky cat poop! Luckily the farmer washes the beans thoroughly, so no poop remains!

Poo, that stinks!

But why drink it? Some say the coffee's flavor is improved when it passes through the civet's tummy. Others say it's tasty because the civet only picks the best cherries. Either way, it's the most expensive coffee in the world! How much would you pay for a cup of cat poop?

RAWR!

Frog Eggs

Your grandparents may remember eating tapioca pudding for school lunches. They might even remember calling it "frog eggs"… With this recipe you can make them a truly memorable dish by serving them ACTUAL frog eggs instead! At least they'll think this yummy goo is real. This version uses chia seeds, which give it an extra-real frog eggs look.

WHAT YOU'LL NEED

- 3 ¼ oz (90 g) chia seeds
- ½ teaspoon vanilla extract
- 1 teaspoon honey or maple syrup
- 20 fl oz (600 ml) milk
- a sprig of rosemary to garnish

serves 4

Making the frog eggs

The chia seeds need to soak for several hours before they are ready to eat, so start this recipe in the morning if you're serving it for dinner or make it before you go to bed and serve it for breakfast.

1 Put the chia seeds in a bowl or divide evenly between four small glass jars.

2 Pour the milk into a jug. Add the vanilla extract and honey or maple syrup and stir together.

3 Pour the milk over the chia seeds so that they are fully covered.

4 Stir together and then leave in the fridge to soak for 3–4 hours or overnight. The chia seeds will absorb the liquid and expand. It will look thick when it is ready.

Add a sprig of rosemary for a "fresh" look!

TASTY TIP

To make frog eggs lemonade, pour lemonade into a glass and top with a spoonful of soaked chia seeds. Serve with straws.

Serving the frog eggs

Once the chia seeds have soaked, you're ready to serve your frog eggs! Serve lovingly with a sprig of rosemary to your grandparents or other honored guest. Watch them cringe in horror when you take a huge, gloopy mouthful! After they've taken a spoonful and the joke is revealed, you can add a tasty topping.

TASTY TIP

Sprinkle any of the following as a topping after revealing the joke: raisins, nuts, strawberries, blueberries, raspberries, orange slices, chopped bananas, mango, seeds, and coconut flakes.

Stinking Fruit

Indonesia

UGH!

Durian is a type of fruit that grows in Malaysia and Indonesia. It's regarded locally as the King of Fruits, but mostly it's known as the world's stinkiest fruit! The durian's smell has been described as "sewage," "stale vomit," and "skunk spray."

The overwhelming stench of durian baffled scientists, so they investigated to see what chemicals it contains. They found over 40 different chemicals, all with distinct, smelly aromas, which—mixed together—make the durian stench. Despite the smell, durian is popular and considered extremely tasty!

The king of fruits

The stinky fruit isn't welcome everywhere, though! It has been banned from Singapore's rail network and is banned on several airlines and in hotels across Southeast Asia due to its disgusting, lingering stench!

Severed Fingers

Greet your friends with your hand wrapped in a "bloody" (ketchup-covered) tea towel, explaining you had a little accident… Tell them that you want to make the best of a bad situation and offer them a fresh, severed-finger snack! They will forgive you when they taste these yummy cheese straws, topped with a tasty almond "nail."

Making the fingers

These tasty, cheesy "fingers" are super easy to make. They keep well in an airtight container, so you can make them several days before you serve them.

1 Grate the cheese and put aside for later.

2 Break the egg into a small bowl and beat with a fork.

3 Put the flour, mustard, salt, and pepper into a large bowl. Cut the butter into small pieces and, using your fingertips, rub the mixture together until it looks like breadcrumbs.

4 Add the grated cheese and half of the egg (we'll use the rest later) and combine to form a dough.

5 Sprinkle a little flour on the work surface. Take small pieces of dough and roll them into 3-in (7-cm) fingers. Put these on a large greased baking tray.

6 Press the centers of each finger together to form knuckles. Using a knife, carefully score lines on the "knuckles."

7 Put in the fridge for 30 minutes so that the fingers firm up.

AARGH!

WHAT YOU'LL NEED
- 4 oz (100 g) aged cheddar cheese
- 1 extra large egg
- 6 oz (50 g) all-purpose flour
- 1 teaspoon yellow mustard
- salt and pepper
- 3 oz (80 g) butter

makes about 20

Adding the fingernails

Once the fingers are firm, they are ready to be baked!

1 Ask an adult to preheat the oven to 350°F (180°C).

2 Using a paintbrush, dab a thin layer of tomato ketchup on the end of each finger where the nail would be. Press an almond onto the finger to look like a nail.

3 Brush the fingers, but not the nails, with the remaining beaten egg.

4 Ask an adult to help you put the fingers in the oven and bake for about 15 minutes until golden brown. Leave for 2 minutes to cool slightly.

WHAT YOU'LL NEED

- a pastry brush or small paintbrush
- 1 tablespoon tomato ketchup
- 20 blanched almonds
- the remaining beaten egg

OOPS!

Making the severed ends

The cheesy fingers look pretty real, but we need that gore factor! Make this rich, tomato sauce to make your severed fingers look 100% authentic. It also makes a tasty dip!

1 Ask an adult to help you finely chop the onion and the garlic.

2 Gently heat the oil in a saucepan. Add the onion and fry for 5 minutes, stirring occasionally. Add the garlic and fry for 30 seconds.

3 Add the tomatoes, tomato purée, chili flakes, sugar, salt, and pepper. Simmer for 10–15 minutes.

4 Use a potato masher to break down the tomatoes to give the mixture a rough texture.

5 Use a pastry brush to dab a thin layer of relish on the end of each finger.

6 Put the rest of the relish in a bowl and serve with the fingers. This can be served warm or cold.

WHAT YOU'LL NEED

- 1 small onion
- 1 garlic clove
- 1 tablespoon olive oil
- 14 oz (400 g) can chopped tomatoes
- 1 tablespoon tomato purée
- $\frac{1}{4}$–$\frac{1}{2}$ teaspoon chili flakes
- a pinch of sugar
- salt and pepper

Bat Soup

Palau

Yes, that's right: bat soup. Bats are eaten regularly in Asian and Pacific countries. They can be enjoyed grilled, deep-fried, stewed, and barbecued. But, on the small island of Palau, it's fruit bat soup which is considered a particular delicacy.

To make the soup, the bat is washed and boiled whole, sometimes with chopped vegetables. Coconut milk is added before the bat is served in a bowl, "grinning" up at the person crazy enough to eat it. Everything is eaten apart from the bones and fur. The meat is torn off the bones by hand, chewed, and then the fur is spat out. Charming!

Are you bat crazy?

Apparently bats taste like chicken. They are high in protein and low in fat, so what's not to like? Well, the smell of urine while you are cooking them can be off-putting, but you can hide this with garlic, onion, chili, or pepper. Or maybe try them all?

Human Brain

This deliciously disgusting human brain cake is perfect for any special occasion. Present it proudly during a dinner party, and your friends and family will think you've gone nuts! They'll be nuts for this yummy chocolate cake too…once they brave a bite!

Making the cake

1 Ask an adult to preheat the oven to 350°F (180°C).

2 Grease a 7-in (18-cm) dome-shape cake pan or oven-safe mixing bowl.

3 Put the butter, sugar, and vanilla extract in a large bowl. Using an electric mixer, ask an adult to help you beat the mixture together until it is smooth and fluffy.

4 Break the eggs into a bowl and beat together. Gradually add the eggs to the butter mixture, whisking all the time, until it is combined.

5 Sift the flour, cocoa powder, baking powder, and baking soda into the bowl.

6 Gently stir with a large metal spoon while adding the milk gradually until combined.

7 Put the mixture into the greased cake pan and gently tap the pan on the countertop to level the surface.

8 Ask an adult to help you put the cake in the oven and bake for about 1 hour or until firm to the touch. Leave the cake to cool for 5 minutes, then turn it out of the pan. Leave to cool on a wire rack.

WHAT YOU'LL NEED

- 7-in (18-cm) dome-shape pan or oven-safe mixing bowl
- 8 tablespoons (115 g) butter
- 10 oz (280 g) light brown sugar
- 1 teaspoon vanilla extract
- 2 extra large eggs
- 8 oz (225 g) all-purpose flour
- 1 ½ oz (40 g) cocoa powder
- ¼ teaspoon baking powder
- 1 ½ teaspoons baking soda
- 8 fl oz (225 ml) milk

serves 8

Making the buttercream frosting

This delicious buttercream frosting will not only taste yummy, it will also keep the cake moist while you decorate it with gooey "brain tissue" later.

1 Cut up the butter and put it in a large bowl.

2 Sift in the powdered sugar and add the milk.

3 Beat with a wooden spoon until smooth. Don't be tempted to use an electric mixer as you will get covered in a cloud of powdered sugar!

4 Using the tip of a skewer, add a very small amount of food coloring to the mixture and mix together to turn the buttercream frosting pink.

WHAT YOU'LL NEED

- 6 tablespoons (85 g) butter
- 2 ½ oz (75 g) powdered sugar
- 2 teaspoons milk
- red gel food coloring
- a skewer

Gooey brains!

Putting it together

This is the really fun part where you get to craft wiggly, gooey brain tissue to stick to the cake and coat it in yummy sticky jelly. You'll be amazed how real it looks!

1 After the cake has cooled, cut out a ¾-in (2-cm) wedge across the top of the cake to make it look like two sides of a brain.

2 Put the cake on a serving plate. Spread a thin layer of buttercream frosting all over the cake and in the cut-out gap.

3 Roll out small pieces of the fondant into ropes about ½ in (1 cm) wide and 5 in (12 cm) long. Using a zig-zag pattern, put the ropes on the cake to cover it. Don't cover the gap you cut out.

4 Brush the jelly all over the cake, putting it into all the lines and the cut-out gap. Splatter some jelly on the serving plate to look like blood.

WHAT YOU'LL NEED

- 1 lb 2 oz (500 g) ready-to-roll pink fondant
- 8 tablespoons seedless raspberry or strawberry jelly

COOK'S TIP

Leave the cake in the fridge for 2–3 hours before carving it to make cutting and shaping it easier. When you do cut it, you can eat the extra pieces. These are the cook's perk!

SERVING SUGGESTION

When you serve the cake to your friends or family, suggest they eat it with their bare hands for an authentic zombie experience.

Sheep's Head

Norway

Do you enjoy lamb chops for dinner? Would you still enjoy them if that cute lamb was staring up at you as a head on a plate? No? Then you might want to avoid Norway and Iceland, where sheep's head is considered a special meal.

In Norway, they call it *smalahove*, which literally means "sheep's head." Originally smalahove was a poor man's dish. Farmers would eat the sheep's head because they couldn't afford to waste any meat. Now smalahove is served as a delicacy in fancy restaurants. To cook, the head is boiled or steamed and served with mashed potato and rutabaga. The eyes are considered the tastiest part and are best eaten first while they're still warm. Yuck!

Heads up!

If smalahove sounds like something you'd like to try, then add it to your Christmas menu. Traditionally sheep's head is eaten the last Sunday before Christmas and nothing gets you in the festive spirit quite like a sheep's head on your plate!

Bloody Intestines

Have you got the guts to serve this gory mass of bloody, red intestines? It may look like a scene from a horror film, but this recipe makes disgusting, stringy intestines out of delicious chocolate bread dough with a scrumptious raspberry and cream cheese filling. So, providing your guests don't faint when you present it, they're in for a tasty dessert!

Making the bread

The squishy intestines are made out of yummy chocolate bread. Be warned, you may end up with red hands!

1 Put the flour, salt, and baking soda into a large bowl. Add the butter in small pieces, rubbing together with your fingertips until the mixture forms fine crumbs.

2 Add the cocoa powder and sugar and mix in. Sprinkle the dry yeast over the mixture.

3 Add the red food coloring to the warm water and stir. Pour into the flour mixture and mix with your hands until it forms a ball.

4 Turn the ball of dough out onto a floured surface and knead for 10 minutes until it is smooth and glossy.

5 Shape the dough into a ball again and put it in a clean bowl.

6 Cover with a clean tea towel and leave to rise in a warm place, like an airing cupboard, for about an hour until it has doubled in size.

WHAT YOU'LL NEED

- 1 lb 10 oz (750 g) white bread flour
- 1 teaspoon salt
- ½ teaspoon baking soda
- 1 tablespoon (25 g) butter
- 1 tablespoon cocoa powder
- 6 oz (175 g) superfine sugar
- 2 teaspoons fast-acting dried yeast
- 2 teaspoons red gel food coloring
- 15 fl oz (450 ml) warm water

makes 24 buns

COOK'S TIP

If you don't want red hands, wear a pair of gloves or ask an adult to help you use an electric mixer fitted with a dough hook.

Making the filling

While the bread is rising, you can make the delicious raspberry and cream cheese filling.

1 Put the raspberries, 2 oz (50 g) sugar, lemon juice, and cornstarch in a saucepan. Ask an adult to help you bring the mixture to a boil.

2 Reduce the heat and simmer gently for 2–3 minutes. Stir frequently, until the mixture thickens. Remove from the heat and let the mixture cool.

3 Put the cream cheese, almond extract, and the 2 tablespoons of sugar in a bowl and beat with a wooden spoon until smooth.

WHAT YOU'LL NEED

- 10 oz (300 g) fresh or frozen raspberries
- 2 oz (50 g) sugar, plus an extra 2 tablespoons
- 1 tablespoon lemon juice
- 1 tablespoon cornstarch
- 9 oz (250 g) cream cheese
- ½ teaspoon almond extract
- 16 in x 11 in (40 cm x 28 cm) stainless steel roasting pan

EURGH!

Putting it together

Once the dough has risen and the filling is cool, it's time to put everything together to make the gory intestines!

1 Grease a large roasting pan measuring about 16 in x 11 in (40 cm x 28 cm).

2 On a floured surface, roll out the dough to a large rectangle, measuring about 24 in x 16 in (60 cm x 40 cm).

3 Spread the cream cheese mixture over the top of the dough, leaving a ½-in (1-cm) gap around the edges. Spread the raspberry mixture over the top of the cream cheese.

4 Roll the rectangle along its longest side into a sausage shape. Cut the sausage into 2-in- (5-cm-) long slices.

5 Gently take a slice, shape it into a loop, and place it in the roasting pan. Continue with the other slices, twisting them, making coils across the pan to look like intestines.

6 Cover with a clean tea towel and leave in a warm place for about 30 minutes to rise again.

7 When the dough has risen, ask an adult to preheat the oven to 400°F (200°C).

8 Bake the intestines for about 35 minutes until beginning to brown. Leave to cool before serving warm, as real intestines would be.

TASTY TIP

While the bread is still fresh and warm, brush over a little light corn syrup to really up the gore factor!

SERVING SUGGESTION

Serve the intestines in the stainless steel roasting pan with a large pair of tweezers to make them look like they have just been surgically removed!

Stinkheads

Alaska

If you enjoy eating fish, then you probably like salmon. The indigenous Central Alaskan Yup'ik people really like salmon and eat it for most of their meals. While you might like smoked salmon sandwiches, however, the Yup'ik people enjoy a different fishy dish called *Tepa*, also known as Stinkheads.

Why are they called Stinkheads, you ask? Well, Tepa is essentially rotten salmon heads. The Yup'ik people are resourceful and so as not to waste any of the fish, they remove the heads from salmon and bury them in wooden barrels under the ground. The fish heads are left there to rot and decompose for several weeks.

A fish out of water

When they are ready, the heads resemble a very smelly mush. Apparently they are very enjoyable, if you can stomach the stench! If not, maybe stick to the sandwiches...

Rotten Eggs

You've never seen eggs like these before: so putrid, so gooey, so...delicious! Turn your Easter celebration into a horror spectacular by serving these "rotten eggs."

Cooking the eggs

1 Put the eggs in a saucepan, cover with cold water, and slowly bring to a boil. Then simmer gently for 10 minutes.

2 As soon as the eggs are cooked, drain and put under cold running water until they are cool.

3 Gently roll the eggs on the work surface to loosen them and to create cracks all over the shells. Don't remove the shells yet.

4 Fill the saucepan with enough cold water to cover the eggs and add a few drops of the green and blue food colorings to make a dark color.

5 Gently add the eggs to the water and leave for 30 minutes.

WHAT YOU'LL NEED

- 6 eggs
- cold water
- green gel food coloring
- blue gel food coloring

makes 6

To make "bloody" eggs use red food coloring!

WARNING

Ask an adult to help you cook the eggs and drain the boiling water. We don't want boiling water splashing you.

Serving the rotten eggs

You've waited patiently—now comes the exciting part. Remove the eggshells to reveal the "rotting" eggs inside!

1 Using a slotted spoon, remove the eggs from the water and dry on paper towels.

2 Gently peel off the cracked eggshells.

3 Put the eggs back in the water for only 30 seconds to give them a final coloring.

4 Your rotten eggs are now ready to be served. That is, if your guests are brave enough to try one!

YUCK!

SERVING SUGGESTION

Why not take your eggs on an Easter picnic? Serve in a ceramic egg container with a blob of mayonnaise on each. Dye the mayonnaise green with food coloring for an extra ghoulish effect! Add to the picnic basket then sit back and enjoy as your picnic quickly descends into chaos!

TASTY TIP

Dip the end of a toothpick in the food coloring and draw extra rotten lines on the eggs for a really gruesome effect. Yuck!

Baby Bird Embryos

Southeast Asia

In parts of Southeast Asia, for example, the Philippines and Thailand, there is a particularly tasty street food enjoyed by many. It is called *balut*.

From the outside, a balut looks like a normal hard-boiled egg, but it hides a gross secret. Crack open the shell and you'll find the developing embryo of a duck, which is eaten whole: goo, bones, feathers, and all! The fertilized eggs are incubated for 14 to 21 days, then steamed or boiled. In the Philippines, diners prefer to eat their balut with a little seasoning: salt and chilli, or garlic and vinegar.

Egg surprise!

Recently, however, balut have gone upmarket, and restaurants are serving them as gourmet food, cooked in omelets or baked in pastry. Very rarely are balut served raw, as this will guarantee an upset stomach! So the next time you are eating a boiled egg, be thankful there's nothing more than yolk in there!

Dirty worm Hash

It's cute when little children make mud pies in the backyard, but your family won't think it's sweet when you serve up this wriggling feast of worms in mud for lunch! They may cringe at first, but they'll be wolfing this delicious chili down after their first bite. No one can resist a hot dog!

GROSS!

Making the dirt

This delicious chili recipe makes a very real looking "dirt" which is perfect for hiding wriggling hot dog worms in.

1 Ask an adult to help you finely chop the onion and garlic with a sharp knife.

2 Carefully heat the oil in a large saucepan over medium heat. Add the onion and garlic. Cook, stirring occasionally, for 10 minutes.

3 Add the cumin, paprika, and chili powder. Cook for 1 minute, stirring constantly.

4 Add the ground beef and cook, stirring frequently, for 5 minutes. Break up any lumps that form.

5 Add the tomatoes, tomato purée, oregano, salt, and pepper then simmer uncovered for 10 minutes, stirring occasionally.

6 Drain the liquid from the can of beans and add them to the beef. Simmer for 2–3 minutes.

7 Keep the chili warming on the stovetop while you make the worms.

WHAT YOU'LL NEED

- 1 onion
- 1 garlic clove
- 1 tablespoon vegetable oil
- 1–2 teaspoons chili powder
- 1 teaspoon ground cumin
- ½ teaspoon paprika
- 1 lb (500 g) ground beef
- two 14 oz (400 g) cans chopped tomatoes
- 2 tablespoons tomato purée
- salt and pepper
- 14 oz (400 g) can red kidney beans

serves 4

TASTY TIP

Add some more chili powder depending on how hot you like your food. Just remember, while you can always add more chili, you can't take it out once it's in!

Making the worms

While your dirt is simmering away and keeping warm, it's time to make your worms. These hot dog worms are delicious and super easy to make.

1 Ask an adult to help you use a sharp knife to cut the hot dogs lengthways into eighths.

2 Put the sliced hot dogs in a large saucepan and pour water over them so they're covered. Bring to a boil then reduce the heat.

3 Cook until the hot dogs begin to curl. Remove from the heat and drain.

4 Remove the chili from the heat and ladle into serving bowls. Add the worms, hanging them over the edges of the bowls and hiding them in the dirt. Serve immediately.

WHAT YOU'LL NEED
- 3 hot dogs
- water

SERVING SUGGESTION

Try serving the chili in new, clean, mini metal buckets to make it look like you've just dug the worms out of the garden!

wasp Crackers

Japan

Your everyday chocolate chip cookies are a bit dull for the Japanese: they prefer something with a bit more of a sting. In the fields near the city of Nagano, Japan, elderly wasp hunters have started making a new delicious snack: wasp crackers! Locally known as *Jibachi Senbei*, wasps are added to a traditional rice cracker (senbei) mix, to make this nightmarish cookie!

Wasp crackers taste OK because the senbei mix contains soy sauce and sugar, giving the crackers a pleasant sweet and savory flavor. It's the texture that is offputting as you bite into the wasps' squishy heads and gooey tummies. You might get the odd crunchy wing or leg stuck between your teeth too...

That must sting!

Before you vow never to try a wasp cracker, it's worth noting how rich in protein they are, making them much healthier than your usual chocolate chip cookie. Maybe you should make the switch? A nice cold glass of milk will wash down those legs and wings easily!

Big Green Boogers

Snot is always foul—it's got a gross-out guarantee! So it's a safe bet that your friends will be horrified when you offer them these giant green boogers as snacks on your next movie night. Take a big handful and gobble them down! Be sure to tell them how fresh they are…

WHAT YOU'LL NEED

- 2 bags microwave butter popcorn
- 7 oz (200 g) sugar
- 6 oz (175 g) corn syrup
- 9 tablespoons (125 g) butter
- ½ teaspoon baking soda
- ¼ teaspoon vanilla extract
- green gel food coloring

makes 1 large bowl

Making the popcorn

1 Cook the bags of popcorn in a microwave, one at a time, following the instructions on the packet. Empty the bags into a large bowl. Be careful of the hot steam!

2 Put the sugar, syrup, and butter in a large saucepan and ask an adult to help you bring it to a boil, stirring all the time.

3 Leave to boil for 5 minutes without stirring.

4 Remove the pan from the heat and stir in the baking soda, vanilla extract, and enough food coloring to turn the mixture mucus green.

5 Pour the mixture over the popcorn and stir together until the popcorn is completely coated.

WARNING

Ask an adult to help you with this recipe: the mixture in the saucepan gets very hot!

Baking the popcorn

Snot comes in all shapes and sizes: round, dry ones; stringy, gooey ones; and blobby, squishy ones! Baking the popcorn makes dry snot with a hint of squish—perfect finger food!

1 Preheat the oven to 250°F (120°C). Grease two large baking trays.

2 Spread the popcorn evenly on the baking trays. Bake in the oven for 1 hour, asking an adult to help you stir it every 15 minutes. Leave the popcorn to cool for 10–15 minutes.

3 Put the popcorn into a large serving bowl or popcorn boxes to serve.

TASTY TIP
Garnish your popcorn with some runny green frosting for a really slimy treat!

YUM YUM

Snot-corn anyone?

Wriggling Octopus

South Korea

The fresher the food, the better it is! That's what we are usually led to believe. Well, food doesn't come much fresher than the South Korean delicacy called *Sannakji* or, if you prefer, wriggling octopus.

Fresh and raw sea food is common in Asian and European cuisines, but sannakji is fresher than fresh. Live baby octopuses (sannakji) are cut into bite-sized pieces and remain wriggling on the plate when served. Not only are they chewy, rubbery, and fairly tasteless, but they are also dangerous...

Now that's fresh!

You see, those wriggling tentacles, while technically dead, still have some life in them and will defend themselves from being eaten! They are covered with powerful suction cups, and as they are swallowed whole, the cups can grab on to your throat, stick there, and choke you. You have been warned!

Bloodshot Eyes Cubes

Just pop a couple of these unnervingly realistic-looking "eyes cubes" in your parents' drinks to start them screaming! These horrifying ice cubes can be enjoyed anytime, but this recipe includes a delicious bloody punch for special occasions.

WHAT YOU'LL NEED
- 15 oz (425 g) can pitted lychees
- a little strawberry, cherry, or raspberry jelly
- 16 large fresh blueberries

Making the eyeballs

Make these creepy "eyeballs" at least a day before you want to serve them, so that there is time for them to freeze.

1 Using a sieve, drain the can of lychees into a bowl. Put the liquid to one side. Place the lychees on several pieces of kitchen paper and leave to dry for 30 minutes.

2 Using a teaspoon, carefully stuff a little jelly into each of the lychees' holes so that they are filled.

3 Gently press a blueberry into the jelly to look like the eyeball's pupil. Repeat for every lychee.

makes 16

Making the ice cubes

You will need to use a large ice cube tray to make sure the lychees fit in the holes.

1 Put the stuffed lychees in the ice cube tray and pour over the leftover liquid from the can to fill the cubes.

2 Put the ice cube tray in the freezer and leave for about 8 hours, or overnight, until ice cubes have formed.

WHAT YOU'LL NEED

- a large 16-holed ice cube tray
- the leftover liquid from the lychee can

Making the punch

Serve the ice cubes in this yummy, bloody punch for a super eerie effect. Or simply add to your favorite cold drink!

1 Pour the cranberry juice and soda water or lemonade into a large pitcher and stir to combine.

2 To serve, turn the ice cubes out of the tray. Pour the punch into glasses and add an ice cube or two to each.

WHAT YOU'LL NEED

- 2 pints (1 liter) cranberry juice
- 2 pints (1 liter) soda water or clear, sparkling lemonade

Put the lychees on cocktail sticks as a garnish!

Fish Eyeballs

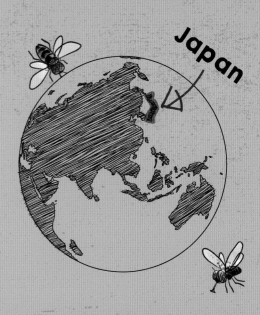

Japan

What is it about eyeballs that make us squirm so much when we think about eating them? Is it the way they look up at you from the plate? Or the thought of them rolling around in your mouth? Maybe it's the idea of them "popping" when you bite down... The thought might make you run for the hills, but fish eyes are considered a cheap and nutritious food in some Asian countries.

In Japan, tuna eyeballs have become a popular dish in recent years. You'll find them on market stalls staring up at you with a cheap price tag of $1 per eyeball. That's good value when you consider how big and full of protein they are!

Surprisingly crunchy!

When you bite through the cornea of a fish eyeball, it is just like eating a grape but more salty than sweet, more fishy than fruity, and more crunchy than slimy. They are very good for you too, especially those from the mackerel family, or so they say. Would you give it a try?

Roasted Mice

The only way to know whether these crispy, delicious snacks are tasty, peppery jalapeños or yucky, dead mice is to brave a bite! Definitely not for the faint hearted!

WHAT YOU'LL NEED

- 4 oz (100 g) cheddar cheese
- 5 oz (125 g) soft cream cheese
- ½ teaspoon ground cumin
- salt and pepper
- 10 large, fat jalapeño chilies with their stems still on

makes 10

Stuffing the bodies

The cheesy filling of these crispy snacks is super tasty, but make sure you don't overstuff the chilies or your mice will have an accident in the oven!

1 Grate the cheddar cheese and put in a large bowl. Add the cream cheese and ground cumin. Season with salt and pepper and mix together.

2 Ask an adult to help you use a sharp knife to slit the chilies lengthwise down one side to make a pocket. Leave the stems on, as these will be the mouse tails. Scoop out the seeds using a small spoon.

3 Using your hands, stuff the cheese mixture into the chilies. Press the cut edges together to seal the filling. Clean any excess cheese off the outside of the chilies with a clean paper towel.

WARNING

When you cut the chilies, do not rub your eyes or let the chilies touch an open wound as the oils in them can burn and sting your skin. Some people like to wear rubber gloves when they cut chili peppers.

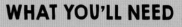

Adding their coats

These spicy chili "mice" have a golden, crunchy coating.

1 Spread the flour on a large, shallow plate and season with salt and pepper.

2 Beat the egg with a fork in a small bowl. Carefully pour onto another large, shallow plate.

3 Put the breadcrumbs on a third large, shallow plate.

4 First, dip each chili in the flour so that it is covered. Second, coat it in the egg and third, roll it in the breadcrumbs until completely coated. Place on the baking tray, with the cut side of the chili facing down.

WHAT YOU'LL NEED

- $3/4$ oz (20 g) all-purpose flour
- salt and pepper
- 1 extra large egg
- $1 1/4$ oz (35 g) panko breadcrumbs
- a baking tray

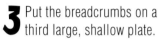

EEK!

Roasting the mice

You can cook the chilies immediately or you can leave them in the fridge for up to a day and cook them when you are ready to serve them.

1 Ask an adult to preheat the oven to 425°F (220°C).

2 Roast the chilies in the oven for 25 minutes, until golden brown. Remove from the oven and let them cool slightly. The cheese can be very hot.

3 While the mice are cooling, use a toothpick to paint two eyes on each mouse with the black food coloring.

4 Use the cream cheese to stick the almonds in place to make ears.

WHAT YOU'LL NEED

- black gel food coloring
- a toothpick
- 20 toasted flaked almonds
- ¼ teaspoon soft cream cheese

SERVING SUGGESTION

These mice can be eaten hot or cold. If you have any leftover cheesy filling, you can use it as a dip to serve with your chilies.

TASTY TIP

If you like really spicy food, leave the seeds in the chilies. It's the seeds that make them hot!

Roasted Rat

Vietnam

Rat is a delicacy in many parts of the world. In Vietnam, for example, rats are considered just as tasty as chicken and easier to come by too!

Rats are frequent pests in rice fields in rural Vietnam, but they are also a great source of protein. Rice farmers kill two birds with one stone when they catch the rats. Not only do they stop them from eating their crops but they also get a tasty meal out of it. The rats in rural areas only eat rice, are free from disease, and apparently taste just like chicken!

Rat popsicle!

Farmers, who used to just eat the rats they caught, are now selling them to restaurants in Ho Chi Minh City and Hanoi, where rat is becoming an increasingly more popular dish because it is considered a "clean" meat. It's served whole, roasted on a skewer, and apparently tastes very sweet! Would you eat a rat popsicle?

Maggot-Infested Brownies

Not many people can say no to brownies, but your friends will scream in protest when you offer them these! In this recipe, fudgy chocolate brownies are topped with a creamy chocolate frosting in which, horror of horrors, maggots are crawling out!

WHAT YOU'LL NEED

- 7 oz (200 g) dark chocolate
- 14 tablespoons (200 g) butter
- 3 extra large eggs
- 1 teaspoon vanilla extract
- 9 oz (250 g) sugar
- 4 oz (115 g) all-purpose flour
- 8-in (20-cm) square cake or brownie pan

makes 12

Making the brownies

These brownies are made with dark chocolate which gives them a rich, delicious flavor!

1 Preheat the oven to 350°F (180°C). Grease and line a square 8-in (20-cm) brownie or cake pan.

2 Break the chocolate into a large, heavy-based saucepan. Cut the butter into cubes and add to the chocolate.

3 Ask an adult to help you to heat the pan gently, stirring the mixture until the butter and chocolate have melted. Remove from the heat and leave to cool slightly.

4 Put the eggs, vanilla extract, and sugar into a large bowl and beat together with a wooden spoon.

5 When the chocolate mixture has cooled, add to the egg mixture and beat together.

6 Add the flour and, using a large metal spoon, fold into the mixture. Pour the mixture into the pan.

7 Ask an adult to help you put the brownies in the oven and bake for about 45 minutes until the top has formed a crust and the center is just set. Remove from the oven and leave to cool.

Making the maggoty frosting

You can never have too much chocolate! Make this terrifyingly tasty maggots in dirt topping for the brownies.

1 Roll the marzipan into a ball and pinch off tiny pieces. Roll each tiny piece into a ball then roll in the palm of your hand to make small sausage shapes. Curl them to look like maggots.

2 Dip one end of the maggots in the food coloring to make the heads.

3 Put the maggots on a plate and leave to dry until you are ready to decorate the brownies.

4 Cut up the butter and put in a large bowl. Ask an adult to help you use an electric mixer and whisk together until the butter is pale and fluffy.

5 Sift the powdered sugar and cocoa powder into the bowl. Add the milk and mix together with a wooden spoon until combined. Whisk until smooth and creamy.

WHAT YOU'LL NEED

- 2½ oz (70 g) white fondant
- black gel food coloring
- 6 tablespoons (90 g) butter
- 5¼ oz (150 g) powdered sugar
- 1½ oz (40 g) cocoa powder
- 2 tablespoons milk

EW!

Putting them together

You have all the parts so now it's time to put them together to complete this nightmarish treat. The brownies keep well for a few days, so you can decorate them now and serve them later.

SURPRISE!

1 Cut the cooled brownies into 12 squares. Using a round-bladed knife, spread the topping evenly on top of the brownies.

2 Scatter the maggots over the top, poking some of them into the topping so that they look like they are crawling out of the brownies.

SERVING SUGGESTION

Pile the brownies into a cookie jar, scattering extra maggots on top of them. When your friend comes to visit, ask them to open it and watch their face fall as they see what's inside!

Maggoty Cheese

Italy

The presence of maggots is usually a sign that food has gone bad, but in the case of Casu Marzu, a cheese made in Sardinia, Italy, live, wriggling maggots mean this cheese is ready for eating...

Casu Marzu is a pecorino cheese—a type of hard cheese made from sheep's milk. To turn it into Casu Marzu, the crust is cut off and the cheese is left in the dark for several months to attract flies. Flies lay their eggs in the cheese, and these hatch into larvae, or maggots. What really gives the cheese its flavor, though, is the maggots' poop, which tastes like gorgonzola. Yuck!

Living cheese!

Live maggots are dangerous to eat as they can chew through the stomach and intestines, which can be fatal. So Casu Marzu must be eaten carefully, ensuring the maggots are chewed to death before they are swallowed. It is no surprise that Casu Marzu is the most dangerous cheese in the world!

Slimy Snail Trails

Gross out your friends with a healthy snack of apple slices covered in fresh and sticky snail slime! Dare them to take a bite and watch them turn as green as the slime! When you've let them in on the joke, you can treat them to a pastry snail to earn their forgiveness.

WHAT YOU'LL NEED

- 14 oz (400 g) can sweetened condensed milk
- 2 tablespoons cornstarch
- 1/4 teaspoon vanilla extract
- green gel food coloring

serves 4

Lemon juice will help stop the apples from browning!

Making the slime

1 Pour the condensed milk into a saucepan and stir in the cornstarch.

2 Ask an adult to help you cook the mixture over a low heat, whisking all the time with a balloon whisk, until the mixture boils and thickens.

3 Remove from the heat and stir in the vanilla extract.

4 Dip the tip of a skewer into the food coloring. Add to the mixture and stir until evenly colored. Add more until the desired color is reached. Set aside until cool.

Putting it together

The slime will keep for several days in the fridge. Put the dessert together just before you are going to eat it, as the apples will go brown soon after you cut them. Snails don't mind brown apples, but humans are often fussier!

WHAT YOU'LL NEED

- 4 eating apples
- 4 fresh mint sprigs

1 Ask an adult to help you prepare the apples. Use a corer to remove the cores and, using a sharp knife, cut the apples into thin slices.

2 Arrange the apples on serving plates and, using a spoon, drizzle the slime so that the apples are well covered. Decorate with a sprig of mint and serve.

Clockwise snails

These delicious pastry snails are perfect to make if you have some leftover pastry trimmings from another recipe. Offer one to your friends after you've horrified them with the slime pudding!

WHAT YOU'LL NEED

- 2 oz (55 g) puff pastry trimmings
- 2 tablespoons chocolate spread
- ground cinnamon to sprinkle

1 Ask an adult to preheat the oven to 400°F (200°C). Dampen a baking tray under cold running water.

2 Thinly roll out the pastry trimmings into a rectangle. Trim the edges so that they are straight. Spread with a thin layer of chocolate spread, leaving a 1/2-in (1-cm) gap at the edges.

3 Roll the pastry along its longest side into a log about 1 in (2.5 cm) wide. Cut the log into 1/2-in (1-cm) discs.

4 Place the discs on their sides on the baking tray, leaving space for them to spread. Sprinkle with a little ground cinnamon.

5 Ask an adult to help you put the tray in the oven and bake for 10–15 minutes, until golden brown. Transfer to a wire rack and leave to cool.

WARNING

Be careful when using food coloring. If you spill it on your clothes or the carpet, it will be tough—maybe impossible—to get out!

Fried Tarantulas

Cambodia

Some people say that the average person swallows eight spiders in their sleep throughout their lifetime... Well, in Cambodia, in Southeast Asia, the average person could eat eight spiders as a single snack!

It is thought that the local people began eating the tarantulas during a time of hardship and hunger, but it has since become a delicacy, regarded by locals as a real treat. If you visit Cambodia, you'll see street vendors with massive woks of fried, crunchy spiders, selling them as a snack. The creepy crawlies are also popular with tourists wanting to try out the extreme cuisine.

Anybody for seconds?

Fried in oil, these hairy spiders have crunchy legs and a soft, meaty head. Only the truly brave will try eating the abdomen, which contains gooey brown stuff made up of the tarantula's guts, eggs, and poop!

Baked Human Hand

This grotesque severed hand will send shivers down the spines of your family when you serve for dinner. It sure looks real, but it's actually a very tasty homemade sausage mixture with apple, cheese, and a juicy onion "bone." Yum!

WHAT YOU'LL NEED

- 1 small onion
- 1 small cooking apple
- 4 oz (100 g) cheddar cheese
- 1 lb (500 g) lean ground pork
- 4 tablespoons chopped fresh parsley
- salt and pepper
- 1 extra large egg

serves 4

Making the hand

When shaping the sausage mixture, make the "hand" large enough to serve four people.

1 Ask an adult to help you prepare the onion. Using a sharp knife, chop the onion finely and put it in a large bowl.

2 Use a corer to remove the apple core. Carefully cut the apple into small cubes and add to the bowl.

3 Grate the cheese and add to the bowl with the pork and parsley. Mix everything together and season with salt and pepper.

4 Beat the egg in a small bowl with a fork. Add to the meat mixture and mix together until well combined.

5 Lightly grease a baking tray. Put the meat mixture on it and shape into a hand. Keep the "fingers" well spaced apart to allow room for them to spread when baked.

TASTY TIP

If you like, you could use lean ground beef instead of pork.

WARNING

Always ask an adult to help when using sharp knives or a hot oven.

Making the nails and bone

It's amazing how easy it is to make food look gross. Who knew that onion could look so much like nails and bone!

1 Preheat the oven to 400°F (200°C) before you start.

2 Using a sharp knife, ask an adult to help you cut the onion in half lengthwise.

3 Press half of the onion into the end of the hand, curved side up, to look like a wrist bone.

4 Carefully cut out 5 nail shapes from a layer of the remaining onion half.

5 Press the onion nails onto the ends of the fingers, shaping them to fit.

6 Put the hand in the oven and bake for 30 minutes.

WHAT YOU'LL NEED

• 1 small onion

SERVING SUGGESTION

Serve with mash potatoes for a yummy dinner! Spread the mashed potatoes on a serving dish and place the "hand" on top.

Finishing the hand

The baked hand will look pretty gruesome at this point, but this step will take it to the next level!

1 When the hand has been baked for 30 minutes, remove it from the oven. Don't turn the oven off yet.

2 Spread the tomato ketchup evenly over the top of the hand. Lay the cheese slices on top of the hand and cut strips of cheese to cover the tops of the fingers.

3 Return the hand to the oven and bake for 20 minutes more until golden brown. If melted cheese has spilled over between the fingers, carefully separate them with a knife.

WHAT YOU'LL NEED

- 2 tablespoons tomato ketchup
- 4 cheese slices

OUCH!

Whale Skin

Greenland

This traditional Inuit dish looks rubbery, feels rubbery, and definitely tastes rubbery! Muktuk is traditionally eaten by Inuit peoples in Greenland, Alaska, and Canada. It is made from whale skin and blubber, which is the fat whales have under their skin.

Muktuk is usually made from bowhead whales, but can also be made from seals or beluga whales. A Bowhead whale could feed an Inuit family for up to a year— that's how big they are!

Tough as boots!

Fresh whale meat is cut into pieces about the size of a sheet of paper and frozen. To serve, it is thawed and diced and usually eaten raw with soy sauce. It is a smelly dish and very chewy! When eating, it is best to chew it thoroughly first which releases oil in the skin making it easier to swallow. Whale skin is as tough as old boots. In fact, they even make boots out of whale skin!

Chewy Cockroaches

Sweet, chewy dates are stuffed with crunchy nuts and cream cheese to make these delicious and squeamishly realistic-looking cockroach treats. Dare your friends to nibble a leg at least, and they'll be rewarded with yummy licorice!

WHAT YOU'LL NEED

- ½ oz (15 g) walnut halves
- 2 oz (55 g) soft cream cheese
- 16 large pitted dates

serves 16

Stuffing the bodies

This is a dirty job, but the sweet, nutty filling is worth it!

1 Ask an adult to help you finely chop the walnuts using a sharp knife. Put the walnuts in a bowl.

2 Add the cream cheese to the walnuts and mix together.

3 With your hands, gently open each date and stuff the dates with the cheese filling. Press the edges together to seal the filling.

4 If there's any excess filling on the outside of the dates, wipe them with a paper towel. It can be messy!

AHHH!

Adding the legs and head

This step will turn those squishy stuffed dates into yucky, scuttling, living cockroaches!

1 Ask an adult to help you cut the cherries into 16 small pieces to make the heads of the cockroaches.

2 Cut the licorice into 6 short pieces approximately ½ in (1 cm) in length.

3 Using a skewer, make 3 evenly spaced holes in each side of the dates.

4 Push the lengths of licorice into the holes that you have made to form the legs.

5 Add a piece of cherry to the end of each date to make the head.

WHAT YOU'LL NEED

- 2 natural-colored glacé cherries
- 8 thin black, purple grape, or cola licorice laces
- a fat skewer

TASTY TIP

Instead of walnuts, you can use other nuts such as hazelnuts, almonds, or brazil nuts.

TASTY TIP

You can use soft preserved dates or fresh dates; both work equally well.

Deep-Fried Rattlesnake

USA

It's apparently bad luck to kill snakes, but this doesn't put off some hungry people, who not only kill snakes, but eat them too! In Texas, rattlesnakes are celebrated every March at the Sweetwater Rattlesnake Roundup where deep-fried rattlesnake is served as the main dish. There's even a rattlesnake eating contest!

Preparing rattlesnake is a risky business. The head is removed first and disposed of quickly because it can still bite after decapitation! The body also still wriggles, making preparation quite tricky! The body of the snake is skinned and the organs are removed, leaving meat and bone ready for cooking.

Crunchy not slimy!

Rattlesnake is cooked by dipping chunks of meat in egg and breadcrumbs before it is then deep-fat fried. It is served with chili sauce to spice up the mild, chewy meat. Do you feel like getting your teeth into it?

Plan a Party

The recipes in this book are perfect for a fun and gruesome party! Turn your birthday into a day of horror by lighting the candles on a brain cake or give the term "finger food" a new meaning by serving a bowl of severed fingers at your Halloween party!

You've been invited to

....

Get the word out to your friends! Tell them what you're celebrating, whether they need to wear a costume, and set a theme—the more gruesome the better! Send your invitations and let the horror begin!

Menu

Draw up a delicious menu to horrify your guests

To start
Roasted mice to heat things up

For the main course
Gorge on baked human hand

To finish
Satisfy your sweet tooth with gooey intestines

Late-night finger foods
Severed fingers washed down with bloody eyes-cube punch

Let's play

Parties aren't parties without dancing and games! Make a playlist of your favorite songs and think of some fun, and preferably gruesome, party games to fill the time when you're not eating!

TIPS AND TRICKS

- Make a shopping list so you don't forget anything
- Do all your shopping a few days in advance
- Move furniture out of the way to make room for dancing and activities
- Make as much of the food in advance as possible

Time to party!

The time has come to welcome your unsuspecting guests to your party of horror... Have fun!

Rules of the Kitchen

A good chef follows the rules of the kitchen. Following these guidelines will make you a better cook and make your recipes even tastier.

Safety first

Cooking can be dangerous, so it's important to always be careful when using sharp knives or when cooking with heat. Always ask an adult to help you with any steps you're unsure about.

• Always use oven gloves when handling hot pots, pans, and trays.

• Always use a chopping board when cutting food using a sharp knife.

• Turn pot handles to the side when cooking on the stovetop to avoid bumping them.

• When stirring pots on the stovetop, always hold the handle firmly.

• Wear shoes while cooking to protect your feet if you drop anything.

Squeaky clean

We only want the food to look gross, not be gross, so it's important to be clean while cooking to avoid any nasty germs ruining the taste of your food.

• Wash your hands thoroughly before you begin cooking, during, and after as well.

• Wear an apron. Aprons not only stop you from getting food on your clothes, they also stop germs from your clothes getting in the food!

• Tie long hair back to avoid any unwelcome additions to your food.

• Wash up your equipment as you go along.

• Keep your work surfaces clean as you cook.

Be prepared

The best chefs are well prepared. A little organization goes a long way to making your food taste better!

• Read the recipe thoroughly before you start cooking so you know exactly what you'll need and what you'll be doing.

• Gather all your ingredients and equipment before you start cooking. There's nothing worse than having to dash out to the store halfway through a recipe!

• If you know you'll have leftover ingredients, make sure you have space to store them or use them in another recipe to avoid waste.

All dry measurements are by weight. A cup of all-purpose flour weighs about 4 1/4 ounces.

Cooking Lingo

Chefs have their own language of cooking terms, which you might not be familiar with. Here are some that are used in this book.

BEAT
To stir or mix ingredients quickly in order to add air to a mixture or to make smooth.

BOIL
To heat a liquid until it begins to bubble and gets very hot. This is the boiling point.

CHOP
To cut food into small pieces with a sharp knife.

CREAM
To mix ingredients together, like butter and sugar, to form a light, fluffy mixture by beating with a spoon.

DICE
To cut food into small cubes with a sharp knife.

DRIZZLE
To pour a very fine stream of liquid over food to decorate it or add flavor.

FOLD IN
To mix ingredients by gently lifting and turning with a spoon. This keeps air in the mixture.

GRATE
To rub food against a grater to make coarse or fine shreds, depending on the holes in the grater.

GREASE
To spread butter or oil onto a tray or dish to stop food from sticking to it.

KNEAD
To work dough by pushing, folding, and stretching it with your hands until it's smooth. This distributes the yeast in the dough to make it rise.

SIEVE
To push a mixture, using a spoon, through a sieve to remove any lumps.

SIFT
To make a dry ingredient finer, such as flour, by shaking it through a sieve to remove any lumpy bits.

SLICE
To cut food into thick or thin pieces using a sharp knife.

SPRINKLE
To scatter fine ingredients, like sugar or spices, over a mixture or finished recipe.

RUB IN
To combine small pieces of fat, like butter, with flour by rubbing together with your fingertips until the mixture looks like breadcrumbs.

WHISK
To beat ingredients, such as egg whites, with a balloon whisk or electric mixer in order to add air s to increase its size.

Index

31901060975929